AF255597

# Money Magic

# A Kids Book Exploring Earning, Saving, and Budgeting While Having Fun!

**Book 1 of the My First Finance Illustrated Book Series**

**Written by Ben Hofstetter and Nick Zehrung**

New Caney, TX

2023

**A book in the Children's Financial Literacy and Learning Path**

Library of Congress Control Number: 2023918045

# Table of Contents

"The most difficult thing is the decision to act, the rest is merely tenacity."

- Amelia Earhart

# Chapter 1:

# What is Money and How is it Used?

# For Parents

Key Themes Explored in this Chapter:

- We discuss what money is used for, primarily for buying things that we want or need.
- The concept of providing value to generate money is explained through doing common household chores to help out the child's parent around the house.

Oh No! We can't buy candy from the store without money!  Not even dressed as a Prince!

*Money is a tool that can be exchanged for things like candy!*

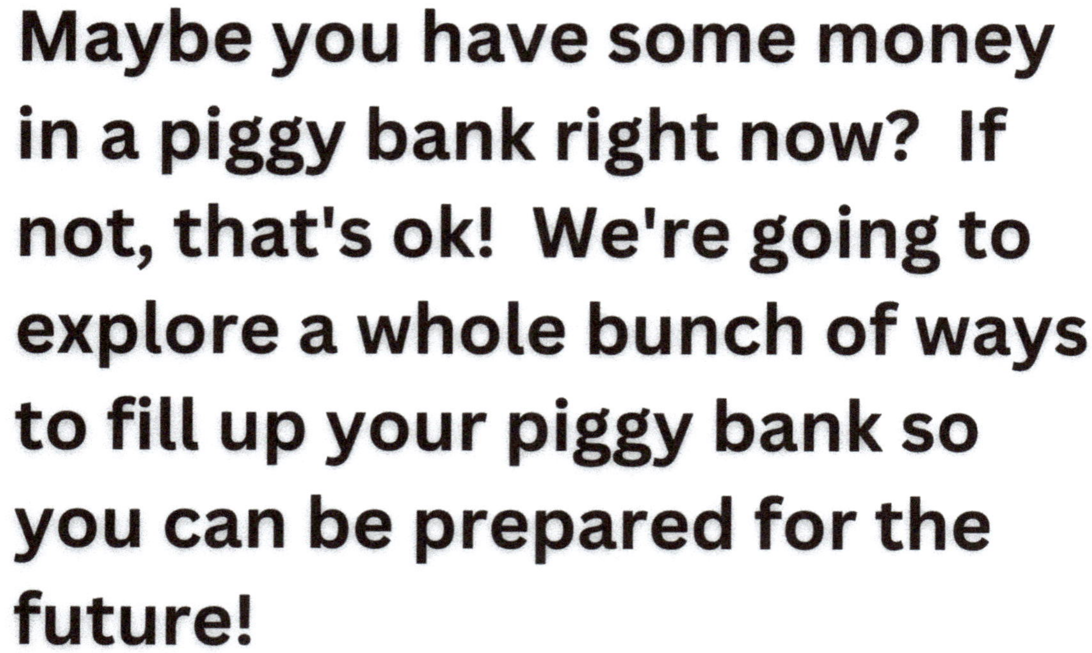

**Maybe you have some money in a piggy bank right now?  If not, that's ok!  We're going to explore a whole bunch of ways to fill up your piggy bank so you can be prepared for the future!**

*Let's start here!  Asking a parent or other trusted family members how you can help make their life a little easier is a great way to Earn your first bit of money!*

*It's always important to ask your parent first and learn how you can help them!*

**Here's a simple idea.  Maybe cleaning up after dinner would be a good start???**

*You could even pretend to be a Prince or Princess while you're cleaning to make it more fun!*

Maybe you and your pet dinosaur can clean your room every day before school???

How about pretending to be a Cowboy and taking your puppy on a walking adventure while getting some exercise!

**Just remember to always be helpful and to always be looking for ways to make someone else's life better!**

*If you do your best and help the team, you'll get rewarded for your hard work, and sometimes that reward will be money!*

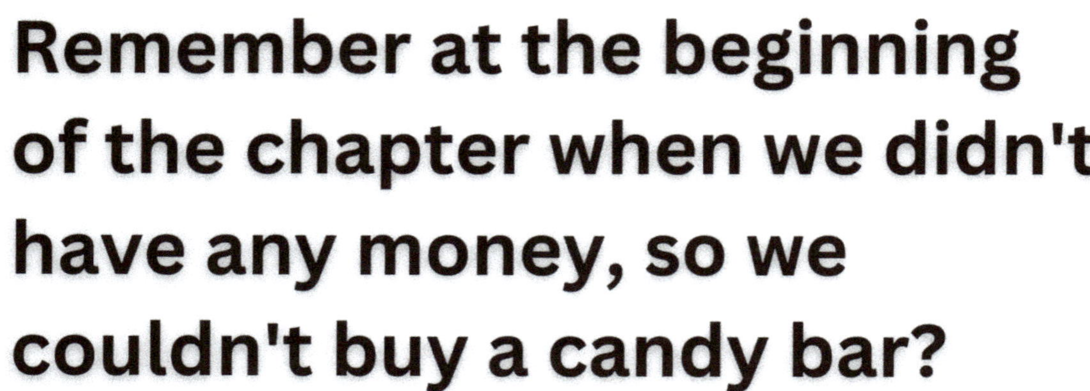

Remember at the beginning of the chapter when we didn't have any money, so we couldn't buy a candy bar?

Well now we know how to earn a little bit of money and we can go get that candy bar, or even upgrade to an ice cream cone!

*In the next chapters we'll explore other ways to use your money that might be even better than candy!*

"If you don't control your money, it will control you."

- Dave Ramsey

# Chapter 2:

# Saving Money Allows For Bigger Purchases in the Future!

# For Parents

Key Themes Explored in this Chapter:

- We start with a short recap on earning money through bringing value to ensure that this crucial building block for the rest of the series has been fully explored.
- We then introduce the concepts of Savings and Delayed Gratification by putting money into a piggy bank to buy a big toy at the end of the chapter, instead of buying a small toy earlier in the chapter.

Like we learned about in Chapter 1, we earn money by providing value to other people!

*When we're young and just starting out, we should be making our Parents lives easier!*

*We can do simple things like cleaning up after playtime to show our Parents that we want to help them!*

Bringing value to the people around us doesn't have to be boring or difficult!  We can make the work we are doing a game to have fun while still helping the people we love!


*Next time you are cleaning up, try pretending like you're a Superhero cleaning up the city after stopping the bad guy!!*

# After earning money we have to decide what to do with it!

*You have a choice to make a small purchase (like an ice cream) now, or Save for a larger purchase (like a toy) in the future.*

Saving our money for bigger purchases in the future is often the best answer!

But where should we put our money before we spend it?

*If you have a Piggy Bank then that would be a great place!*

*If not, you can make one yourself with a shoe box!  Just cut a small hole in the top big enough to fit some paper money and coins in, and you'll have your own Bank that you can decorate however you want!*

**Here's a secret we'll learn about in the next chapter. Sometimes magic happens while money is stored in a safe location, and more money is created without additional work!**

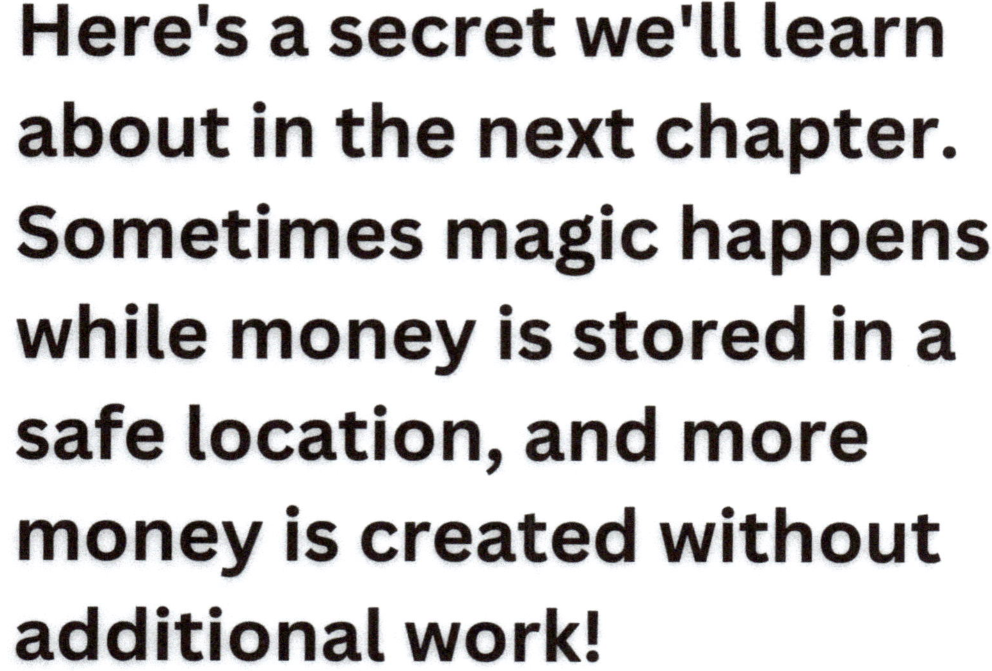

*This only works if we're saving our money instead of spending it though!  So make sure you start practicing sooner rather than later!*

After we have been putting our money into our Piggy Bank for a while, it will start to get full! This is when we'll know that we've saved enough for a big purchase!

*Saving money, instead of spending it right away, allows you to buy items that cost more than you make from doing only one chore!*

*Maybe after a couple weeks you can buy a new Video Game or Toy that you've been wanting!*

Buying big toys, like a Monster Truck,  wouldn't have been possible without saving money in the piggy bank!

"A penny saved is a penny earned."

- Benjamin Franklin

# Chapter 3:
# Saving Money and Using a Magic Piggy Bank!

# For Parents

Key Themes Explored in this chapter:

- Saving in a checking account (or cash) is good for having money very quickly, but it doesn't generate additional funds automatically. This theme is explored through placing cash earned from chores into a wallet.

- Putting savings into a High Yield Savings Account generates money automatically (through interest), but it takes slightly longer to get the funds into a position to be spent. This theme is explored by using a magical piggy bank that generates extra money while we sleep.

- Starting a money saving habit is better than spending on unnecessary things because the greatest asset to building wealth is time.  So the earlier your kids start saving the better they will be.

We know that we make money by bringing value to other people, and we learned that saving money is good, but what are the easiest places to actually put our money once we earn it?

*The easiest places are either our wallet or our piggy bank!*

*In the previous chapter we discussed putting the money we earn into our piggy bank, but in this chapter we'll see that it's a good idea to keep a little in our wallet too!*

We put money into a wallet when we want to be able to use it instantly! This doesn't mean you have to, but it gives you the option!

*You may have heard of a bank account before, a bank account and a wallet are almost the same thing in the grown-up world!  Only instead of having paper money, your money is stored in a bank and you can see it online!*

*This makes your money harder to lose, or accidentally leave in your pockets to go through the washing machine!*

**Having your money in a wallet (or a bank account) is very safe and you can spend that money just as fast as you can find your wallet!**

**It's good to have a little bit of your money in your wallet so you can make quick purchases, but it's not the best place to keep most of your money!**

*Next we'll look at a way to store our money so that it's constantly be growing!*

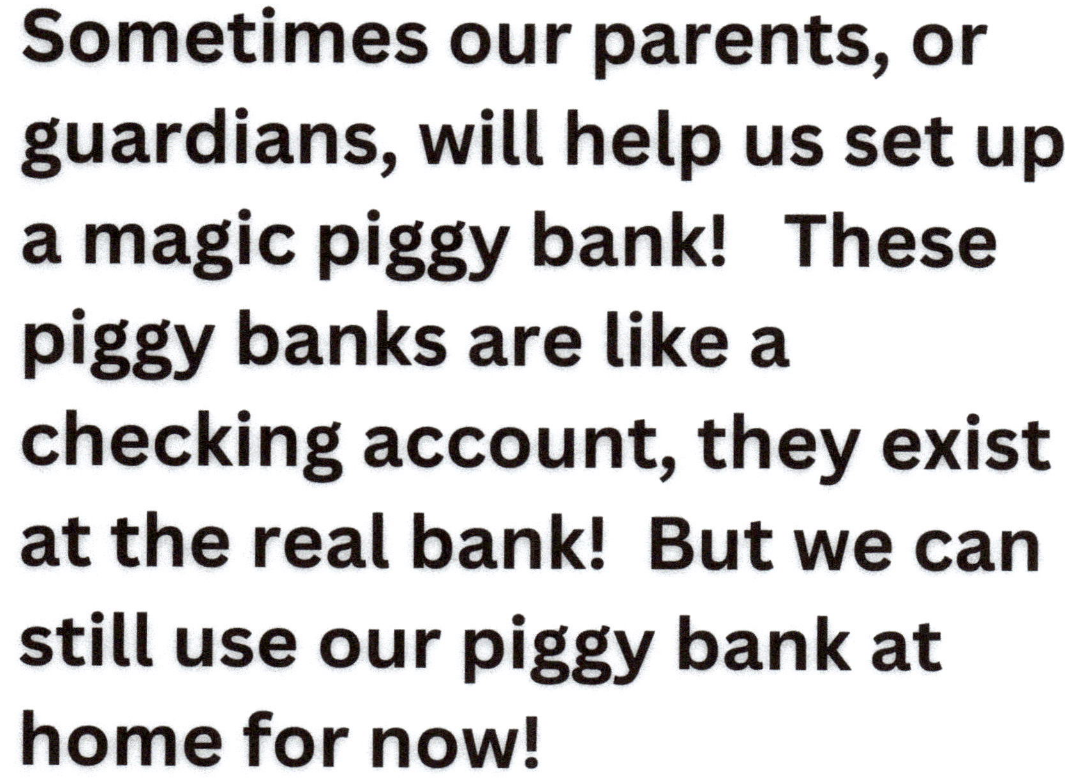



*These are called High Yield Savings Accounts to grown ups, but for now we'll just call them magic piggy banks!*

When your money is inside a magic piggy bank it's always growing, even when you're asleep! This is a slow process, but it doesn't take any work from you!  The only thing you have to do is put the money in the piggy bank!

*When you're young, your magic piggy bank won't seem like it's giving you much money, but as you get older the magic piggy bank will earn you lots of money for free!*

**There's an important difference between a magic piggy bank and a wallet that we haven't discussed yet; the magic piggy bank takes a little bit more time to get your money out of!**

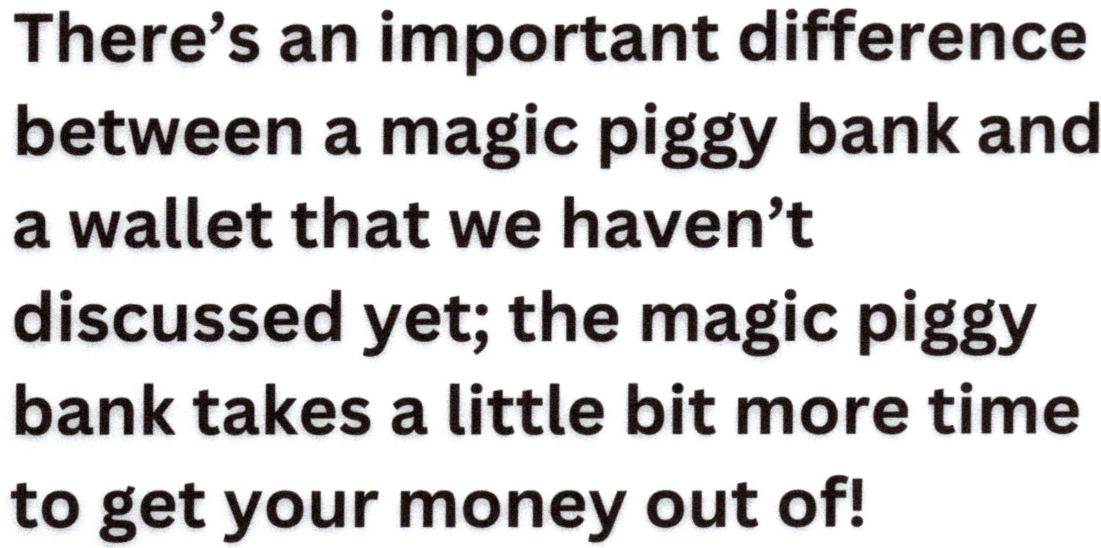

*Think about your piggy bank at home. To get the money out, you might have to open a small hole on the bottom and dig the money out in a slow process! But with your wallet, the money is very easy to grab!  This is also true with the magic piggy bank!*

*This isn't a bad thing!  It's just important to remember for the future!*

Remember, it's good to have some money in your wallet for quick purchases like ice cream, but it's even better to keep most of your money in a magic piggy bank. That way, it's always working hard to make more money for you!

"Budgeting is the first step toward financial freedom. It empowers you to take control of your money and build a solid foundation for your future"

- Suze Orman

# Chapter 4: Using Budget Magic to Buy a Bike!

# FOR PARENTS

Key Themes Explored in this chapter:

- We discuss the basics of saving for a specific reason or purchase, and explore this concept through saving to purchase a bike.

- We learn about a simple budget (income - expenses), and how budgets can be created.

- We discuss how it's important to understand how much money is left over at the end of a period of time (a week in this analogy), and then how we can allocate those leftover funds to saving for a big purchase, like a new bike.

Saving up for a big purchase like a bike can seem hard, but it's easier than you think! You just need to make a plan, and that plan starts with a budget.

*Budgets are extremely important to learn as you grow up!*

The first thing you need to know is what your income is in a certain period of time. For example, your weekly income is the money you earn from doing chores every week!

*You need to know how much income you have so you can plan how much money you can save.*

**The next thing we need to know is what our expenses are. Expenses are things that we spend our money on!**

*Maybe you like to buy gum or a new toy every once in a while, these would be examples of expenses!*

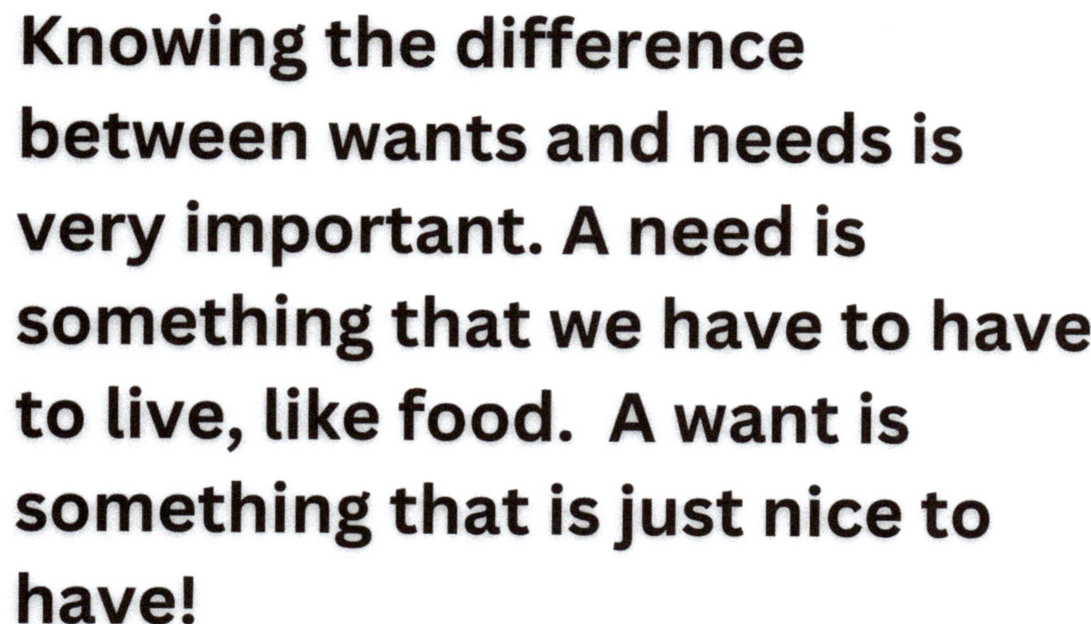

**Knowing the difference between wants and needs is very important. A need is something that we have to have to live, like food.  A want is something that is just nice to have!**

*Wanting something, like a new toy, just because our friends have them is probably not a good reason to buy it! It's important to remember to save our money and only buy things we've really thought about!*

*Sometimes it's okay to buy things just because we want them.  We just need to make sure we don't do it very often!*

**Now it's time to do fun math! Take your income and then subtract your expenses.  The remainder is called your Savings!**

**If the number is positive, then congrats you have money left over to save for the future!**

*If the number is negative, that's ok! You just need to work on earning more money and spending less money throughout the week until you get it right!*

Now that we have our Income, our Expenses, and our Savings, we can finish out building the budget!

The goal of the budget is to show $0, because that means we know where all of our money is going each week!  Here's an example!

*If you make $10 a week (income), and you spend $3 a week at the school vending machine (expenses), then you would have $7 a week for savings!  So your budget would be:*

*$10(income) - $3(expenses) - $7(savings) = $0 (Great Budget!)*

*This would be a perfect budget!*

Now that you know how much money you save every week, you can calculate how long it will take until you can buy that bike!

*For example, if you save $7 a week, and the bike costs $70, then it will only take you 10 weeks to save enough to buy the bike!*

Now you know how to build a budget and why it's important! Building a budget will help you save money for things you really want, like a bike!

*With a little planning and discipline, you'll be able to buy that bike in no time!*

Thank you for reading Book 1 of the My First Finance Illustrated Book Series!  We hope it generated some great ideas as you teach your children about the world of personal finance!

Look out for Book 2 of the series where we discuss bringing value to your community to earn money!

If you enjoyed this book, we have a series of coloring books published titled the "My First Finance Coloring Book Series" which can be found on Amazon! The concepts follow the same pattern as this book, but are written for a younger audience. There are plenty of fun pictures to color, along with a few activities!

You can also follow us on Instagram for more great content and activities to try at home!

Reach out to us with questions at
www.myfirstfinancebook.com